REAL SEA MONSTERS

by Geraldine & Harold Woods
Illustrations by Norman Nodel
Cover by Myron M. Morris

NUTMEG PRESS

© 1979 Shelley Graphics Ltd.
Published by Nutmeg Press,
   a Division of Shelley Graphics Ltd.
Printed in the United States

ISBN 0-89943-025-2

REAL SCARY SEA MONSTERS

SCARY SEA MONSTERS

It was a beautiful day for a race. The boy in a small rubber boat with a tall sail was happy. He was far enough ahead of his friends to enjoy a comfortable lead. Suddenly, a huge creature rose out of the water. The side of the boat was in the monster's mouth. The boy screamed in terror as the beast came closer and closer . . . and stopped.

"Cut!" yelled the director. "We'll have to do it over again." The film crew groaned. Their 25-foot mechanical shark, star of the movie *Jaws II,* was all tangled up in its wires again.

The fake shark of the Jaws movie is the latest, and probably the most famous, sea monster to scare people all over the world.

But it is by no means the first. Ever since they began to swim and sail, people have been afraid of the creatures who lived in the water. They have been amazed by their size and strength. And, both awed and fearful of their dangers. They told tales about strange monsters — a sea serpent as long as a city block, for example, and a creature whose back was so wide that it was sometimes mistaken for an island. Sailors told stories of terrifying attacks by these monsters. There was an octopus-like creature that was supposed to have sunk an entire fleet of ships with its powerful arms. And a beast with six heads that gulped down a sailor with each of its mouths.

Scientists have usually considered such stories about sea monsters as entertaining, but untrue. But nobody really knows for sure. At present only about one twenty-five millionth of the oceans' depths have been explored. And since there are about 300 million cubic miles of ocean, there is more than enough room for even the largest monster to hide.

Some evidence has come in to support the tales and stories. One expedition, for example, lowered a 3-foot iron hook into the sea. The sailors felt a tug on the line, and then nothing. When they reeled in their hook they were shocked. Something had been strong enough to bend a 3-foot iron hook and escape! Another expedition found an eel larva 6 feet long. If this larva were to grow at the same rate as a common eel larva, the adult eel would reach a length of 70 feet.

The sea still holds many secrets. But some of the creatures we do know about are strange enough or big enough to really deserve the title *monster*. Like the beast that weighs over 100 tons and eats 4 tons of food a day. Or, the one with eyes as big as basketballs. Or, the fish that can ram its bony snout through several inches of metal and wood. These are only a few of the *real* sea monsters we know about so far. They don't always live up to the ancient legends, but they are scary enough to start a few new legends of their own!

SHARKS —

THE SWIMMING MOUTHS

The shark is one of the most feared creatures on earth. It is a real-life sea monster, and an ancient one as well. Its ancestors first appeared in the ocean about 350 million years ago. Teeth almost half a foot long have been found from some of

these ancient sharks. To have teeth that size, the shark's mouth must have opened wide enough to allow a man to stand upright in its jaws. Scientists believe that these ancient sharks may have reached a length of 60 feet.

In their present form, sharks have existed for about 60 million years. This means that the sharks we see today have hardly changed during the last 60 million years. There are about 250 kinds of modern sharks. Some are only 4 inches long, and some are as long as their ancestors. But no matter how big they are, sharks are still scary.

Tooth Factories

Sharks would qualify for the title *sea monster* with their teeth alone. Many kinds of sharks, for example, have an average of 3,000 teeth in their mouths. The teeth are set up in five or six rows, one behind the other. Unlike human beings, sharks can replace lost teeth. When one falls out, a tooth in the row behind it moves up to take its place. Sharks lose teeth so often that they could be called *tooth factories*. A single shark may use up to 20,000 teeth in a ten year period!

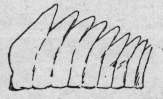

Shark teeth

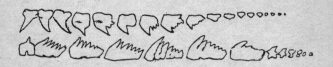

Some shark's teeth are several inches long, and razor sharp. Others are jagged or flat. Surprisingly, the two largest types of sharks have no teeth at all! The Whale Shark and the Basking Shark, which reach 60 feet in length, eat nothing but tiny plants and animals that float in the sea. Instead of teeth, these sharks have strainers in their mouths. The sharks swim with their mouths open, taking in sea water. They catch tiny plants and animals, called plankton, in their strainers.

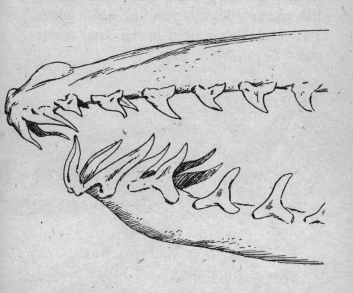

The Great White Shark

The most dangerous shark is the Great White Shark. It is also called the White Shark and the White Pointer. This shark received its nicknames — man-eater, white death, and death shark — for good reason. It has killed more human beings than any other type of shark. Most are about 20 feet long, but White Sharks have been known to reach 40 feet. The White Shark has 3-inch long, razor-sharp teeth, and it can swallow fish and animals up to half its length whole. The shark that starred in the *Jaws* movies was a Great White Shark.

Super Swimmers

All sharks have strong tails and stiff fins. Most have streamlined, cigar-shaped bodies. But no shark has a single bone in its body. Instead, sharks' skeletons are made of a strong, bendable material called cartilage. We have cartilage in the tips of our noses and in our ears.

Streamlined, bendable, strong — these facts about sharks make them good swimmers. And in fact, sharks have been clocked at up to 40 miles per hour for short distances. It's lucky that they are good at it, because most sharks have to spend *every*

minute of their lives swimming, even while they are asleep! This is because sharks "breathe," or take in oxygen, by passing water over their gills. Other fish can pump water over their gills by opening and closing their mouths. But sharks can not do this. So they swim with their mouths open, forcing water back to their gills. If they stop swimming, they will not get any oxygen!

The Tiger Shark

The Tiger Shark is feared and avoided because of its attacks on human beings, par-

ticularly in Australia. It lives in warm waters, and is usually 12 to 18 feet in length. The Tiger Shark gets its name from the stripes it has when it is young. Older Tiger Sharks are gray with only a very faint pattern of stripes on their backs.

15

A Swimming Nose

For all their strength and speed, however, sharks do not appear to be too smart. Even the largest sharks rarely have brains over 3 inches long. But in spite of their small brains, sharks are sensitive creatures. A line of nerves on each side of their bodies senses waves, depth, and water currents. With this information, sharks can tell if a fish or boat is in the water, even if they can not see it. Sharks' eyesight, however, is good enough to see objects 100 feet away. Sharks have also been called *swimming noses*. They can detect *one part of blood mixed with one million parts of water!*

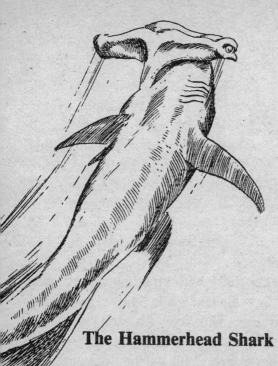

The Hammerhead Shark

Truly the strangest looking shark is the Hammerhead. Hammerheads have wide, T-shaped heads with eyes and nostrils on each end of the T crossbar. The head of a Hammerhead can be 3 feet from tip to tip, and the body can be as long as 15 feet. Hammerheads are found all over the world. They rarely attack human beings.

The Saw Shark

Another shark with an oddly shaped head is the Saw Shark. Saw Sharks have long pointed noses with teeth on each side which they use to cut up their food before eating. Saw Sharks are small — they measure less than 3 feet long — and do look exactly like saws!

The Swimming Mouths

Instead of being called *swimming noses*, sharks might better be called *swimming mouths*. The Whale and the Basking Sharks eat tiny plants and animals. The natural food of other sharks is all kinds of fish, shellfish, and sea lions. But sharks seem to eat just about anything that comes in their path. A license plate, a roll of roofing paper 30 feet long, telephone books, pots and pans, a bottle of wine, and a keg of nails have all been found in the stomachs of sharks.

The shark's wide-ranging appetite has also been the cause of at least two trials. In 1799, the captain of an American ship sailing in British waters was arrested by British officers. He was suspected of trading with the French, which the British considered a crime in those days. Before he was captured, the captain threw all the papers that had evidence against him overboard. Unfortunately for him, a shark ate the papers. The shark was caught by fishermen and cut open. The papers were brought to court and the captain was judged guilty. In another case, a tatooed human arm was found inside a shark's stomach. Doctors who examined the arm quickly realized that it had not been bitten off by the shark. The tatoo on the arm was traced, and police found that the tatooed man had been murdered. Using the evidence found in the shark's stomach, police were able to solve the case.

Sharks will often eat other sharks. On occasion, they will even eat parts of themselves. This happens during a feeding frenzy. In a feeding frenzy, a large group of sharks

are drawn to wounded fish or animals in the water. The presence of food and other sharks eating seems to make the sharks wild. They thrash around, snapping at the food and at each other. In their confusion, sharks turning too quickly will begin to eat their own tails.

The Thresher Shark

Thresher Sharks are known for their long tails, which measure about half their length. Threshers up to 20 feet long have been found. They use their tails to slap the water and frighten schools of fish. The fish then swim close together, and the sharks swallow them all in one bite. One Thresher was even seen throwing fish into his mouth with his tail!

A Man-Eater?

Many people saw the movies *Jaws* and *Jaws II* and began to be fearful of sharks. But the fear of sharks is a lot older than that. As long as people have been aware of sharks they have felt sharks were dangerous, man-eating monsters.

But sharks do not really deserve such a bad reputation. Only a small portion of the 250 types of sharks have ever attacked human beings at all. And those who have attacked people have often done so because they were trapped, sick, or wounded. One shark attack, for example, occurred when a shark could not get out to sea because a sandbar was in its way. Because it was low tide, there was not enough water on top of the sandbar to allow the shark to swim over it. The shark may have attacked because it was afraid and wanted to defend itself.

Other sharks have attacked people when their natural instincts were triggered by a swimmer's behavior. Skin divers with wounded fish in their belts, for example, sometimes draw sharks with the smell of blood. Bathers splashing around can also attract sharks, because the fish that sharks usually eat splash around when they are hurt. It is perfectly natural for a shark to look for an easy meal. Sharks are also attracted to silvery ornaments, perhaps because they resemble certain types of fish.

Of course, not all shark attacks can be explained. There is no known reason for some incidents. People who swim in waters inhabited by sharks are usually advised to stay in a group, and to avoid swimming at night. No one should swim with an open wound, and shiny jewelry should not be worn in the water. But no matter how they act, most swimmers are in little danger. Very few people are attacked by sharks. In fact, each year more people die in the United States from bee stings than die from shark wounds in the entire world!

WHALES — "THE LORDS OF THE SEAS"

Blue Whales are the largest mammals that have ever existed on earth. They are much bigger than the great dinosaurs were. A Blue Whale can weigh more than 100 tons. Its tongue alone, is the size of an elephant. The

Blue Whale's lungs weigh as much as a ton. It takes seven strong men to drag a Blue Whale's 1,000-pound heart across the deck of a whaling ship.

Their fantastic size makes Blue Whales incredible animals. In addition, their strength has inspired quite a few legends. Blue Whales have been known to drag a boat as great a distance as 50 miles. Their tails can inflict damage. And, they are believed to have sunken ships just by accidentally running into them.

Giant Animals, Giant Appetites

Surprisingly, such a huge mammal does not have any teeth. Like the largest sharks, it has a series of strainers in its mouth. It feeds on plankton, the tiny plants and animals that float in the water. A Blue Whale traps large quantities of water in its mouth with lips that are 5 feet high. It then releases the water and the plankton get caught in the strainers. The strainers, called baleen, are 10 feet long.

A favorite feeding ground for Blues and other whales is off the coast of South America. This is a particularly good spot for plankton. During the summer months there is so much plankton there that the ocean appears to be covered with a rusty red carpet several miles across and 30 feet thick. The cold water in this part of the ocean has more oxygen and carbonic acid than warm water does. This helps the plankton grow. There are also many upswelling currents in this part of the ocean. These currents bring food from the bottom of the ocean to the surface, where plankton feed. There is a similar spot near the North Pole, though it is not as fertile as the plankton-filled southern waters. For this reason, northern whales are not as large as southern whales.

When Blue Whales go to their feeding grounds they eat a fantastic amount of food. They eat almost nothing all winter, when they are in warmer waters. Then they gorge themselves during the summer months, making up for lost time and preparing for the winter to come. When a Blue Whale is feeding it eats about 4 tons of plankton a day. It is hard to believe that there is enough food in the oceans to feed these large whales. But there is enough — with plenty left over. Each year the ocean produces about 200 million tons of krill alone. And krill is only *one* type of plankton.

Land Animals in the Water

A Whale is not a fish, even though it lives in the water. It is an animal whose ancestors lived on land. For reasons no one knows, about fifty million years ago a number of animals moved from the land to the sea. As the centuries went by the whales' bodies changed to make living in the water easier. Their legs became fins, to help them swim. When scientists cut up the fins of whales they can still see bones that used to be fingers. Whales also lost their outer ears. They were not necessary to hear under water. And of course, whales became larger. An animal living on land could never become as big as a whale. Can you imagine the size of the legs it would need to walk? In the water it does not matter how large a body is. It can still float. Because of their immense size whales can stay warm. Their blubber is like a blanket that warms them as they swim in cold water. A Blue Whale might have 20 tons of blubber wrapped around it.

It might seem strange that something which spends most of its time underwater has to breathe air. In adapting to living at sea, the way whales breathe has changed. When a whale is under water it has to hold its breath. Its nostrils are on the top of its head. They reach the surface first when the whale rises. Most whales go to the surface about every 5 minutes for a breath of air. Some whales can hold their breath over an hour.

The first sight of a whale is usually what appears to be long spouts of water being shot into the air. The spout is actually stale air being forced out of the whale's lungs. Each whale has a different type of spout. A Blue Whale's spout is about 25 feet straight up into the air. Some whales spout backward and others have more than one spout. A whale that spouts forward is the Sperm Whale.

Today, seals and polar bears are doing what whales did centuries ago. Both animals' bodies are slowly changing as they spend more time in the water. Perhaps, in a couple of million years they will have completely moved into the sea as whales have.

The Humpback and the Right Whale

Whales fall into two categories: baleen whales, that eat by straining their food, and toothed whales, that kill for their food. Most

of the larger whales are baleen. The baleen whales include the Humpback and the Right Whale, as well as the Blue Whale.

The Humpback is the most playful of the baleen whales. Often sailors see them jumping high out of the water and landing with a great splash. During mating season they are often observed playing with each other. They like to give loving pats to their friends. Their pats are gentle for whales, but the slaps can be heard several miles away.

The Right Whale has had the unfortunate reputation throughout history of being easy to hunt. Unlike most whales, it floats after it is killed. This made it possible, and much easier, to hunt Right Whales before modern techniques in whaling were developed. The Right Whale got its name from being the "right whale" to go after. Now with modern techniques and equipment, other whales are the "right whales" to hunt. Some of the larger whales are endangered. There are laws to limit catches, but many people would like stronger laws. And others would prefer to see an end to whaling.

Sperm and Killer Whales

Sperm Whales are not like Blues. They have teeth and are used to fighting. They are the only known animal on earth to take on the Giant Squid and win. A typical Sperm Whale has large scars near the mouth. They are left there by squid who try to get away as

they are eaten alive. There are also many cases of Sperm Whales fighting back and sinking boats with whalers trying to catch them.

Sperm Whales are killed for their oil and blubber. In the head of a Sperm Whale there are 10 to 15 barrels of an oil known as spermaceti. Spermaceti is used to make the best candles. It is also used to oil machinery. Sperm Whales are also the only source of a

substance called ambergris which is used in making perfume.

Another whale that has teeth is called the Killer Whale. It lives up to its name, although it is not close to the size of the larger whales. Killer Whales are only about 30 feet long. But their razor-sharp teeth are so well-known that some of the larger whales merely roll over and give up when they are attacked by a pack of Killers.

Killers are also choosy eaters. They sometimes kill a Gray Whale just to get its tongue. Whalers are not interested in catching Killers. They sometimes prove annoying by tearing large pieces of flesh from whales that have been harpooned. But sometimes they have also helped whalers. There have been reports of Killer Whales herding other types of whales to the whalers' boats. They are rewarded when the whalers cut the tongues out of the mouths of the captured whales and give them to the Killers to eat. When they finish, they go out and find another whale to herd to the whalers. Killers usually ignore human beings in the water. The few attacks that have occurred may have been the result of mistaken identity. The Killers may have thought the person was a seal, or a penguin.

Can Whales Talk?

Scientists are now only beginning to understand how well whales can communicate with one another. They think that whales can hear one another hundreds of miles away. Humpback Whales repeat long complicated song-like noises. Sperm Whales can cause avalanches in the mountains found under the sea with their loud voices. Communication is apparently important to whales for mating and feeding. The large number of ships with their noisy engines possibly interfere with the "conversations" of whales.

No one is sure if these voices are merely the whale's means of finding other whales, or if these giant animals are actually talking to each other. If they actually are talking, the possibility exists of human beings learning the language. Then we could "talk" to the whales too. This exciting possibility is now being studied by scientists.

The songs of whales have fascinated people throughout history. Sailors of long ago used to tell stories of their ships "singing" in the dead of night. Needless to say the singing was quite a mystery and formed the basis of many seafaring tales. It is now known that the songs were caused by vibrations in the water. The voices of whales are so strong

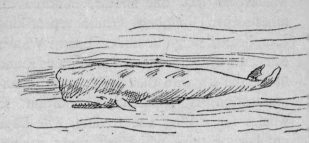

that they are capable of making ships vibrate and seem to sing songs.

The whales, or the "Lords of the Sea," have always amazed human beings. They are truly remarkable creatures.

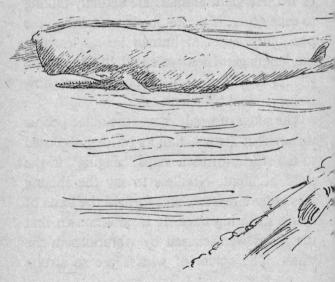

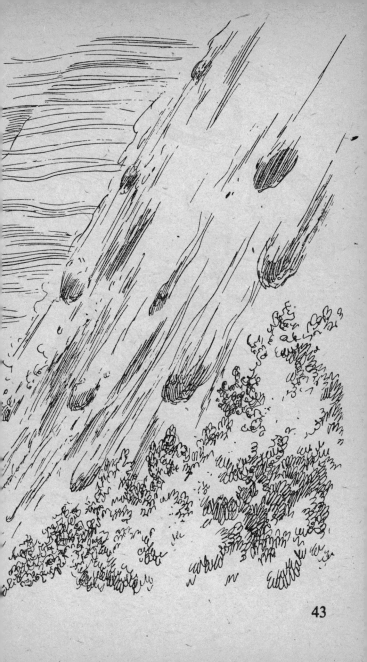

GIANT SQUID —
BIGGER GIANTS?

On October 26, 1873, two fishermen were in a small boat off the coast of Newfoundland. A twelve-year-old boy was with them. As they sailed for home after a hard day's work, the fishermen saw a strange, flat object in the water. They moved in for a closer look and poked the object with a boathook. To their shock, the "thing" suddenly became a mass of huge, waving red arms. Each arm was covered with suckers. The fishermen screamed as one arm gripped the boat and began to pull it under. But the young boy grabbed an ax and swung it with all his might. The ax hacked and sliced right through the arm, and the creature disappeared into the ocean, leaving its arm still wrapped around the boat. The fishermen returned to shore and measured the arm. It was 19 feet long.

The animal that attacked the fishermen was a type of squid. There are over 300 kinds

of squid. Most are about a foot long, and some are smaller than a dime. The largest squid, such as the one that attacked the fishermen, are called Giant Squid.

An Ancient Sea Monster

Sailors all over the world have told stories about giant sea monsters with many limbs. An ancient Greek poem, the *Odyssey*, men-

tions a monster with six heads and twelve feet. This monster was called Scylla. The hero of the poem, Odysseus, sailed his ship too close to Scylla. She reached over and ate a sailor with each of her mouths.

Many generations of Norwegian sailors also told tales about giant sea monsters. They called these monsters *krakens*. Krakens had many arms and were said to be a half a mile across. According to the legends, sailors would land on a kraken's broad, flat back, thinking it was an island. They would even build campfires and settle down for the night. Unfortunately, after a few hours the kraken would decide to swim away. The unsuspecting sailors would then be dumped in the ocean.

In the early 1800's, a Frenchman wrote about a giant creature with many arms that sunk an entire fleet of ships. Many more sightings were reported on the Norwegian coast in the 1870's. In spite of all these stories, most scientists did not believe that Giant Squid really existed. They thought that people who said they saw such creatures were imagining things. The sightings along the Norwegian coast in the 1870's, for example, were said to be the result of drinking too much of a new kind of rum that had become popular about that time.

But, a few years later, scientists received proof that there was at least some truth to the tales about many-armed monsters. For some reason, Giant Squid began to be washed up on shore. For the first time, Giant Squid could be studied carefully.

A Head-Footed Giant

What they found was strange indeed. The Giant Squid reaches a length of almost 60 feet. Most of its length is made up of eight arms and two longer tentacles. These limbs are often as long as a three-story building is high! They are covered with suckers. Suckers can hold on to things, and can also taste and feel. The squid's arms grow directly from its head. Giant Squid are members of a group of animals called Cephalopods. Cephalopod means "head-footed." Octopuses are also members of the Cephalopod family.

Giant Squid have completely soft, boneless bodies. They are covered with a thick, protective skin called a mantle. Inside the mantle is a small space. Squid move by taking water into this space and then squirting it out again. The water is squirted through a structure that looks much like the nozzle of a garden hose. The squid can change direction by aiming the nozzle.

Giant Squid are usually brick red in color. This seems to be a strange color for a sea

monster, yet it helps to protect the squid.
Giant Squid live deep in the ocean where
there is little light. In the underwater dark-
ness, red coloring looks black. So the squid
is hidden in the blackness of the water.

If this were not enough camouflage, squid

can also send up a smokescreen! The smokescreen is really made of ink. The ink allows
the squid to swim away unobserved and also
acts as a decoy. The ink hangs in the water as
a dark shape. Many attackers think the ink is
their prey. While they are busy trying to cap-
ture it, the squid makes a clean getaway!

In the center of the Giant Squid's head is a huge beak. It looks like the beak of a parrot. When the squid eats, it holds its prey with its arms and pecks at the prey with its beak. Squid have no teeth in their beaks, but they do have teeth in their tongues. Squid tongues are tough, elastic ribbons. They scrape and tear off bits of food. Giant Squid also have huge eyes. They look a lot like the eyes of a human being. The only difference is that they are as big as beach balls!

A Bigger Giant?

Giant Squid are not large enough to live up to all the legends told about sea monsters. But there is some evidence that the Giant Squid we now know of have cousins — cousins whose size could make our "giants" look like dwarfs.

Giant Squid are hunted by the Sperm Whale. When a Sperm Whale fights a Giant Squid, the squid leaves sucker marks on the skin of the whale. A 50-foot squid leaves a sucker mark that is 4 inches in diameter. But sucker marks over *18 inches* in diameter have been found on whale skin. To leave a mark that wide, the squid would have to be about *200 feet* long. That would be about as long as *ten* average-sized automobiles parked one behind the other! Also, pieces of squid tentacles as thick as a man's body have been found in the stomachs of Sperm Whales.

A Gentle Giant?

No one has yet seen one of these huge creatures. But as we become more skilled in exploring the oceans, the chances of finding a "giant" Giant Squid increase. Luckily, the Giant Squid that have been seen so far usually leave human beings alone. Attacks are rare and usually occur only when the squid has been attacked. The Canadian fishermen, for example, were in no danger until they poked the squid. Another famous attack occurred after a squid was shot at by a rifle. This happened in 1874. Passengers on a ferryboat sailing to the Indian city of Madras were horrified to see a Giant Squid drag a small boat under water. The Captain survived to explain what had happened. He had seen a Giant Squid fighting with a Sperm Whale. After a while the squid broke away

from the whale and began to swim for safety. The Captain fired a few shots at the squid. To defend itself, the squid sank the boat.

SEA MONSTERS
THAT POISON

Not all monsters are huge creatures with powerful muscles. Some of the most dangerous animals in the sea are small and weak. But they have a weapon that protects them against attacks by sharks, squid, and even people — poison.

Stonefish

There are many creatures in the sea whose bite or sting is poisonous. The stonefish is probably one of the most dangerous. It is

definitely the ugliest! Small and chunky, the stonefish is slimy and covered with warts. It lies on the ocean floor, half buried in sand or mud. When it does this it looks exactly like its namesake, a stone. In fact, visitors to aquariums often walk away from a tank containing several stonefish complaining that the tank is empty.

Unfortunately, stonefish are not as harmless as the rocks they resemble. They have thirteen spines on their backs. These spines are sharp enough to cut through the sole of a sneaker. When the spines stab a victim, glands at the base of the spine squirt poison into the wound. This poison causes terrible pain, and has been known to kill people. One victim of a stonefish who lived to tell about it was Doctor J. L. B. Smith, a scientist who studies fish. One day, Doctor Smith was stung in his thumb by a stonefish he had captured. He survived, although he suffered intense pain for several hours. He also reported that his entire hand was weak and sore *three months later*. An interesting effect of stonefish poison is that it changes a person's sense of hot and cold. Ice, for example, feels hot to a victim, and boiling water, cold.

Luckily, doctors have now found an antidote to stonefish poison. This won't help the unsuspecting creatures of the sea, however, who swim too close to the stonefish's hiding place and get stabbed by a spine. Most of them die quickly. But surprisingly, the stonefish does not use its poison to hunt food. It saves this powerful weapon for defense against enemies.

When it comes time to look for a meal, the stonefish relies on speed. For something that looks like, and most of the time acts like, a rock, the stonefish is incredibly fast. When a smaller fish swims by, the stonefish opens its mouth, springs forward, and gulps the fish down. Then it settles down in the mud again. Scientists at the New York Aquarium filmed and timed this whole process. The stonefish spent exactly *one-sixteenth of a second* catching the fish, eating it, and returning to the bottom for its after-dinner rest!

Zebrafish

Another good fish to stay away from is the zebrafish. The zebrafish is also called the turkeyfish, the lionfish, and the red-fire fish. It looks something like a Fourth of July parade. Only a foot long, the zebrafish has gay, maroon-and-white stripes, and a large assortment of decorations. Each of the zebrafish's huge fins, for example, has fifteen separate rays fanning out from it. The zebrafish's head is adorned with twelve tabs of skin, which flutter like flags as the fish swims.

But, some of this beauty is deadly. On the zebrafish's back are thirteen sharp spines. There are three more underneath the fish,

and two behind. Like the stonefish, the zebrafish uses these spines to inject a dangerous poison into its victims. This poison, however, is not as deadly as stonefish poison. Victims of zebrafish poison suffer great pain for several hours, but they do not die.

Zebrafish like to fight. If anything threatens them, they put their heads down and aim the thirteen spines on their backs at the offender. The zebrafish does not seem to get frightened, even if its opponent is many times its size. Once some adult zebrafish were seen getting ready to eat their young. The small zebrafish, only a few inches long, prepared themselves for a counterattack. The adults decided to leave them alone!

The Blue-Ringed Octopus

Many people are afraid of octopuses. They see the creatures' eight arms, each lined with suckers, and shudder. Most octopuses, however, are quite harmless. In fact, most octopuses seem to be much more afraid of people than people are of them! When they see a human being, octopuses usually scurry away.

Surprisingly, the only really dangerous member of this family is the tiny Blue-Ringed Octopus. The Blue-Ringed Octopus measures only 4 to 6 inches across. It gets its

name from the blue rings that decorate its orange body. Blue-Ringed Octopuses are mostly found in Australia. They are responsible for a number of deadly attacks on people who picked them up.

The Blue-Ringed Octopus has a beak like its relative, the squid. It pecks at its victim with this beak, and injects a drop of poison into the wound. Since the octopus's beak is so small, most people do not even realize they have been bitten until they feel dizzy. By then it is too late. The Blue-Ringed Octopus, so tiny, so unexpectedly dangerous, is one animal to stay away from.

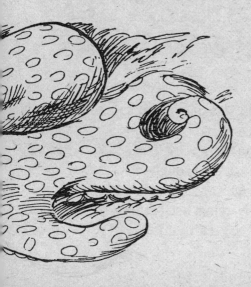

AN ASSORTMENT OF MONSTERS

Can you imagine a fish so skinny that it can't be seen head on? Or one whose snout is a dangerous weapon? Then there's the fish with a mouth big enough to swallow a Volkswagon, and the creature who escapes its enemies by tying itself into a knot. All of them are real sea monsters.

Barracuda

No one can make a list of dangerous fish without including barracuda. There are over twenty types of barracuda, but the Great Barracuda is the most feared. In Florida it is more feared than sharks. An adult Great Barracuda can be over 6 feet long and can weigh about 100 pounds. Barracuda are very thin fish — so thin that it is next to impossible to see them when they are swimming straight at you. This is why the barracuda's victims often do not know what hit them. All they get is a glimpse of a silver streak darting away after the attack.

Scientists think that many reported shark attacks are actually the work of barracuda. One way of telling what type of fish has struck is by inspecting the wound. The barracuda has a very long jaw. The jaw is filled with razor sharp, double-edged teeth. When a barracuda bites into something, the slash is very neat. The wound does not have the jagged appearance of many shark bites. Also, most barracuda attacks result in a single wound. Barracuda move in very quickly, tear off a piece of flesh, and move on. Occasionally, however, barracuda do attack twice.

Barracuda attack their prey in two different ways, depending on the size of the victim. Small fish are usually swallowed whole. Often, when a recently killed barracuda is cut open, four or more fish will be found in its belly without a scratch on them. Larger prey are usually torn in two by the barracuda's knife-like teeth. Each piece can then be gulped down.

There is no doubt that barracuda are man-eaters. There have been a number of proven attacks on human beings. But there have also been many instances of men swimming untouched through barracuda-infested waters. Divers often report having been followed by barracuda. They find it annoying, but not always dangerous. The barracuda are apparently only interested in what appears to them to be a strange-looking fish. Jacques Cousteau, the famous explorer of the ocean world, tells of the time he was caught right in the middle of a school of barracuda. There were so many fish that he could not see beyond the silvery wall. Oddly enough, he simply dropped beneath the school of fish and swam away. He considers himself a lucky man.

Why do barracuda sometimes attack and sometimes ignore human beings? It seems as if they think they are making a meal out of another type of fish when they strike people. This argument is supported by the fact that most barracuda attacks on human beings occur when the water is cloudy. When the water is not clear, the barracuda can not see as well. And while sharks encircle their victims a number of times before striking, barracuda just rush in, take a bite, and leave. They could easily make a fatal mistake.

Another theory is that in cloudy water barracuda are attracted by metal objects which swimmers might be wearing. A shiny watch or chain might resemble a silvery fish.

Swordfish

Willis Blount considers himself a lucky man. He harpoons swordfish for a living, and he does not have any unusual scars on his body. So far he has had only one close call. He had just harpooned a swordfish. Instead of rolling over and dying, it leaped out of the water. Its sword missed him by only a few feet. It caught him by surprise, for that is not how the average swordfish gets back at its pursuer. Swordfish usually strike from underneath. Those that still have some fight in them after they have been harpooned, slam their huge swords through the bottom of boats and slash unwary fishermen in the legs. Willis has many friends with long scars on their legs and feet. But Willis is a cautious man. Whenever he sees a swordfish charging, he stands on a seat in his boat. There is less chance of the sword reaching him there.

Swordfish can be found in warm and temperate oceans throughout the world. Off North America, they swim as far north as Nova Scotia during the summer months. Swordfish are one of the oldest creatures to inhabit the earth. Scientists estimate that they have been around for 100 million years. Perhaps one reason for the remarkable age of the species is the number of eggs the female produces in a year. Between June and September each female lays between 10 and 100 million eggs. Many of these eggs never hatch, but just a small percentage would insure another generation of swordfish.

Also, once a swordfish becomes an adult it does not have to worry too much about being killed by other fish. Perhaps very large sharks and Killer Whales are the only sea creatures that have a chance in a battle with a swordfish. Two fishermen once watched an hour-long battle between a 25-foot shark and a swordfish. The swordfish won. Another time a fisherman caught a swordfish off the coast of Massachusetts. Attached to its sword was a 125-pound Blue Shark.

Swordfish grow surprisingly large. The average weight of an Atlantic Swordfish is between 100 and 300 pounds. Many are caught that weigh much more than that. Every year a few weighing 500 pounds or more are taken in by fishermen. The largest ever was caught off the coast of Chile. It was

15 feet long and weighed an amazing 1,182 pounds.

The most noticeable thing about the swordfish is its sword. The sword takes the place of the teeth found in other animals. Swordfish have no teeth at all. When hunting, the swordfish sticks its sword, which can reach a length of 4 feet, into a school of smaller fish. It wildly slashes them to pieces, and then goes back and eats the remains. A sea captain once saw a swordfish flail

through a school of herring. After the swordfish left, he was able to scoop up a bushelful of dead herring left over from the swordfish's meal.

There have been many reports of swordfish attacking boats. These attacks were recorded since the beginning of history. The ancient Greeks and Romans wrote about them over 2,000 years ago. One attack occurred in 1828. The ship was a whaler. The swordfish slammed into the ship and put a hole in a cask of oil stored inside the ship. In order to reach the cask, the sword had to go through a layer of copper sheathing, an inch of undersheathing, a 3-inch plank of hardwood, a board of solid white oak timber and another 2½ inches of hard oak!

Even modern vessels are subject to swordfish attack. In 1967 a research submarine, the Alvin, was forced to surface after being attacked by a swordfish at a depth of 1,800 feet. It made a direct hit on one of the view windows and eventually became wedged between the hull and the outside covering of the sub.

Swordfish attack for many reasons. The most obvious is self-defense. Some people think that they accidentally ram ships while chasing other prey. Other people claim they simply have bad tempers.

Moray Eels

Moray eels have a problem. They like dark, shadowy places. They usually live in holes found in the coral reefs of tropical and sub-tropical waters. They also live in the cannons of sunken ships. Their problem is that their bodies can grow up to 8 feet long. When somebody disturbs their resting place, it is impossible to get their long, 100-pound bodies out of danger quickly. So, the moray eels are forced to attack.

Fortunately for the eels, they have an adequate defense — their teeth. They have several rows of teeth in their upper jaw and two in their lower. These teeth are long and sharp. Although they usually only hunt for food, a moray disturbed by a diver can inflict a bite as severe as a barracuda's. In

many ways, a human being attacked by a moray eel is in greater danger than a barracuda victim. The barracuda strikes and then swims away. It's not so simple with a moray. They bite and hold on. It is next to impossible to get a moray to release its hold once it has bitten. The diver's only defense is to chop off the head of the eel. Even after that is done, the diver will still have to pry open the clamp-like jaws.

There are over twenty different types of moray eels. They are usually colored very brightly, which makes it hard to see them

against the colorful reefs. The most common variety of moray appears to be green. It is actually blue, but its skin is covered with a yellow slime. The combination gives the eel a green appearance.

One of the moray eel's habits makes it look particularly scary. Morays like to stick their heads out of the hole they are in and continuously open and close their jaws. This exposes their sharp teeth. What the moray is actually doing is forcing water through its gills. What it seems to be doing is warming up for the next battle.

People think that the moray is more vicious than it actually is. Perhaps it is the moray's feeding habits that give it such a bad reputation. During the day, morays sit in their holes, and at night they search for food. Morays love octopuses. If a moray eel comes across a small octopus it swallows the octopus whole. But if the octopus is larger, the moray takes a bite. Then it goes back for more. Slowly, the octopus is eaten alive.

The only defense the octopus has is to shoot out a jet of black ink. Surprisingly, it is not the blinding power of the ink that confuses the moray. The ink actually disturbs the eel's sense of smell. Morays rely on smell more than sight. Once the water is filled with the black ink the moray can not smell the octopus. Hungry morays have been seen bumping into octopuses in ink-filled water and not even noticing them.

An octopus would be making a mistake if it tried to grab onto the moray. When a moray is being held, it ties itself into a knot. It then slips its body headfirst through the knot, thereby freeing itself from the octopus's grasp.

Even when they are given food that they do not have to fight for, their eating habits make morays seem more bloodthirsty than they really are. When morays in an aquarium are fed, they grab large pieces of food and smash them until the water is filled with little pieces of food. Once, two morays went for the same piece of food. One missed and smashed the head of the other. Incidents like that make people have second thoughts when they are told that morays are not very dangerous if they are left undisturbed.

Not all fish are afraid of morays. A very small type of fish called wrasse swims alongside the eels. It swims around the moray, taking its food off sores and parasites that live on the eel. It even goes inside the eel's mouth and picks the moray's teeth! For some reason, the wrasse's behavior does not bother the moray. Wrasse actually feed in the jaws of death!

Groupers

For years, pearl divers off the coast of Australia told stories of fellow divers being swallowed alive by Giant Groupers. Along the waterfront of San Juan people spoke of groupers waiting under the dock for someone to dive in. Shell divers in the Orient claimed to have been stalked by groupers, in the same way cats stalk mice.

More recently, a United States Navy lieutenant reported narrowly escaping being swallowed by a grouper. His oxygen tanks made him too large for the grouper to swallow. A pearl diver off the coast of Australia claimed to have an even closer call. The grouper closed its mouth around the diver, but the man escaped by swimming through one of the fish's huge gill openings.

Until recently, scientists dismissed such stories as the product of wild imaginations. They continued to write about groupers as being shy and afraid of humans. One of the reasons scientists found it difficult to believe the man-eating grouper tales is that no one could produce any evidence. The slash marks on a shark or a barracuda victim were instant proof that these fish were not friendly. But it is not so easy to prove that a grouper has attacked a human being. A grouper never leaves a trace of evidence.

Groupers attack their prey in a bloodless manner. They simply open up their huge jaws and create a suction that draws the victim into their mouths. There have never been any proven fatal attacks on a human being. But some people have been classified as missing who swam in grouper-infested waters. And modern ocean exploration has revealed that groupers are much larger than previously thought, quite large enough to swallow a human being in one gulp.

Groupers get larger as the water they live in gets deeper. The Nassau Grouper weighs 50 pounds. The Giant Grouper which inhabits the waters off Florida and South America can weigh up to 750 pounds. The Queensland Grouper which lives near the Great Barrier Reef in Australian waters may weigh up to 1,000 pounds. There are probably groupers in the deeper parts of the ocean weighing more than a ton. A diver working off an oil rig in the Gulf of Mexico reported seeing one big enough to swallow a Volkswagon.

Groupers are very difficult to spot under water. They hide in the shadows of rocks, reefs, or sunken ships. To make them even harder to find, they have the ability to change colors instantly. In a matter of minutes, a grouper can change from blue to bright yellow with black polka-dots. A Nassau Grouper has been observed completely changing its color eight different ways.

The body of a grouper sometimes has lumps under the skin. The lumps are the remains of sharp-tailed eels. Sometimes they are still fighting for freedom when they reach the grouper's digestive system. If they break through the grouper's stomach with their sharp tails, they eventually die in the grouper's body cavities and become mummified. Their mummies remain forever buried in the grouper's body without harming it.

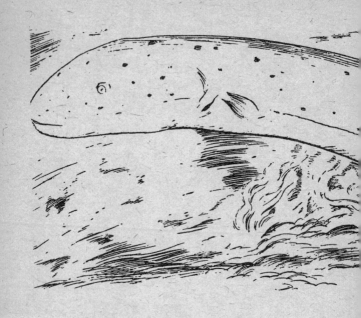

OTHER
WATER MONSTERS

Strange monsters are not only found in the deep waters of the ocean. Rivers also have their share.

Electric Eels

Electric eels, for example, live in the dark, muddy waters of some South American rivers. Although they share a name, electric eels and moray eels are not related to each other. This is because electric eels are not really eels, but fish. One of their distant cousins is the common goldfish.

An electric eel might be a good animal to have around during a blackout. This strange creature contains about 500,000 electroplates in its body. These electroplates produce up to 650 volts of electricity — more than enough to kill a human being. However, the eels do not usually generate that much power. Instead, they discharge about 40 or 50 volts. This is enough to light up a light bulb placed in an aquarium tank.

Electric eels are brown in color, with patches of orange on their heads and throats. With their long, rounded bodies, electric eels look a little like thick "live wires." Most are 3 to 6 feet in length, but electric eels can reach a length of 9 feet. Only one-fifth of the eel's body contains organs for eating, taking in oxygen, reproducing, and performing other bodily functions. The rest of the eel's body produces electricity. Eel's bodies are well-equipped to survive attacks by other creatures. If the end of the eel's body is bitten off, the eel is usually able to grow a replacement.

Eels need their electricity to stay alive. A young eel can see, but an adult eel is blind.

Electricity helps the eel to locate prey in the water. While the eel swims, it gives off a weak electric charge. The charge bounces off fish and other water animals, and is sensed by special organs in the eel's head. Once its prey is located, the eel stuns it with an electric shock. An electric eel's charge is strong enough to paralyze a frog that is 3 feet away. Electric eels may also use electricity to communicate with each other. Although they are blind, eels know when another eel has discharged electricity and killed its prey. When one eel begins to eat, all the nearby eels come over for a free handout. Electricity is also the eel's defense against attacks by larger creatures.

Most of the time eels only shock people. The real danger is that the eel's shock will stun people and cause them to drown. Since water conducts electricity, people in water near an eel can receive a shock even if they have not actually touched the animal. People in South America who want to cross an eel-infested river often send a cow in first. After the cow's body has absorbed the shock, the people can safely enter the water.

Piranhas

Piranha is an Indian word which means *tooth fish*. The Indians could not have picked a better name. Anyone unlucky enough to come across a piranha in the water will remember only one thing about it — its teeth!

Sometimes piranhas travel in schools of fifty or sixty. No one bitten by fifty or sixty piranhas could live to tell the tale. It would take a school of piranhas only about two minutes to clean every scrap of flesh off a human being.

Piranhas only live in a few rivers in South America. Much of this area is jungle, where few people live. Scientists thought the natives were telling tall tales about the deadly fish in their rivers. They did not really believe the stories of people falling off canoes and being eaten alive. But slowly the scientists came around. The evidence of the fish's man-eating reputation could not be ignored. One time, for example, a film crew watched a 400-pound hog in piranha-filled waters being reduced to a skeleton in only a few minutes. The crew caught the savage attack on film. As they filmed it, they could not help imagining how the piranhas would act if *they* went in for a swim. No one volunteered!

There are about twenty types of piranhas, but there are only about four that attack large animals. The most vicious is the Black Piranha. Piranhas eat mostly fish. The presence of blood in the water drives them into a feeding frenzy. Like sharks, piranhas will take large bites of flesh out of one another during a frenzy. Curiously, these bites do not bother a piranha much, and they can adapt to this savagery. Within a week, the large wounds which a piranha has received during a feeding frenzy will completely heal.

Though their wounds mend quickly, piranhas still have to be careful in the presence of their fellow piranhas. They fight over who owns which piece of territory. If two piranhas are put into an aquarium one will eventually kill the other, to prove that he "owns" the aquarium. If three are put together, two will gang up on the other, and then the remaining two will fight it out to the finish. Six is the magic number. Six or more pirahnas in an aquarium will live happily together. Each piranha is too wise to take on the other five. So they have to accept each other's presence.

Candiru

Surprisingly, the earth's real vampires do not wear long capes and attack when the moon is out. In some of the same rivers of South America where piranhas live is a little-known and rare fish called the *vampire catfish*. It is known as *candiru* by the natives of the region. Like vampires, candiru bite into their victims and suck out every drop of

blood they can get. They are only about 2 or 3 inches long and look like little eels. But after a meal of their favorite food — blood, they become large and fat. Small fish die from the vampire's feast, but larger fish allow them their meal of blood and ignore them.

Schools of vampire catfish become very hungry when a warm-blooded animal enters the water. The native Indians have learned to

keep their cattle out of candiru-infested waters. After crossing a river where vampire catfish live, a cow has a life expectancy of about two hours. When the body of a cow that has been attacked by a number of candiru is cut open, only the smallest trace of blood can be found. In two hours, the candiru can drink every drop of blood in a cow's body. They are truly vampires.

Naturally people are cautious and stay away from these river waters. The tiny vampire monsters have prickly spines on their bodies, which makes it difficult, if not impossible, to pull them out. The only thing that helps at all is a plant called *xagua* that grows in Peru. Candiru do not like the taste of xagua, so if the victim is given some, the fish will eventually leave the victim's body. The presence of such water monsters — whether candiru or piranha — is enough of a warning to guarantee that no one goes for a swim.

THE LAST WORD ABOUT *REAL* SCARY SEA MONSTERS

Millions of years ago our animal ancestors left the ocean to make a new life on land. Now, protected in submarines or equipped with modern skin-diving gear, human beings are returning to explore the world beneath the sea.

The creatures of the sea often seem strange or scary to us. But no doubt whales, if they could read, would find a book about how people get food or defend themselves frightening also. They might even decide to call such a book *Real Scary Sea Monsters!*

There are many more interesting fish and animals in the oceans and rivers of the world. To describe them all would take a book several feet thick! And as ocean exploration continues, even more strange creatures will be discovered. These creatures may seem like monsters to us, but they are simply behaving in a natural way. They are dangerous, yes. But it is important to remember that in the ocean world *we* are the invaders.